This Book Belongs To

_____

_____

_____

Color Test Page

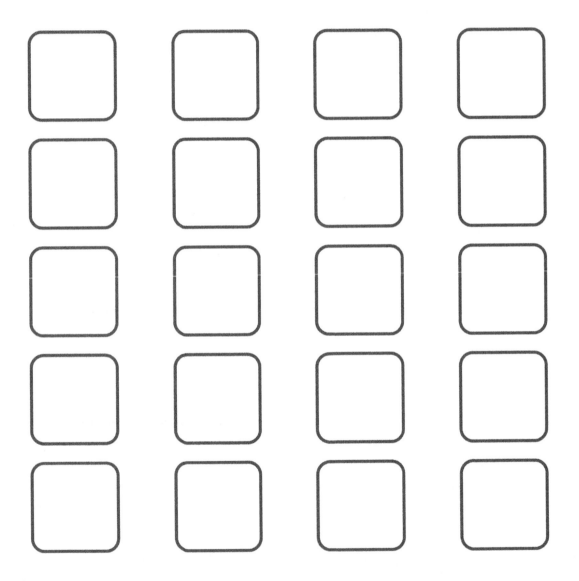

Apricot

Cucumber

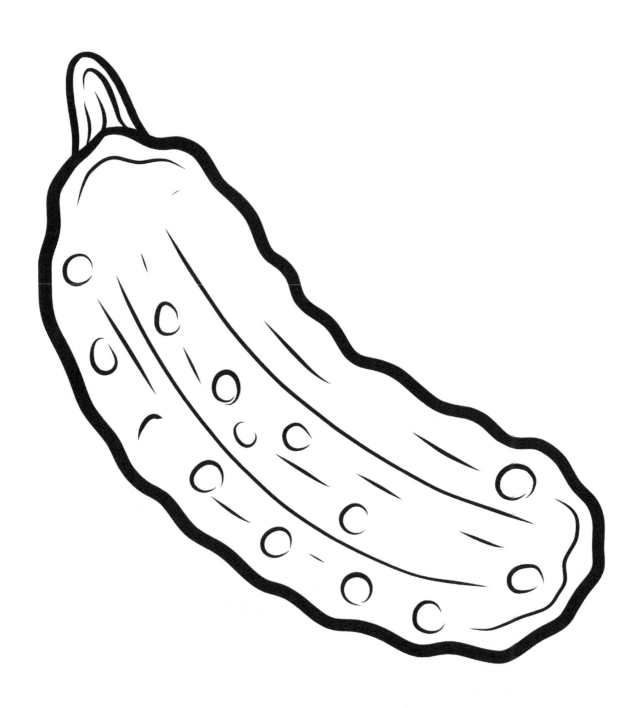

Papaya

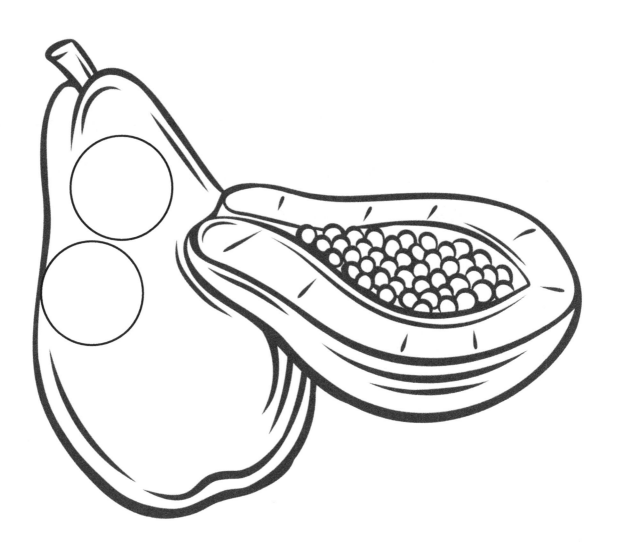

Tomato

Mango

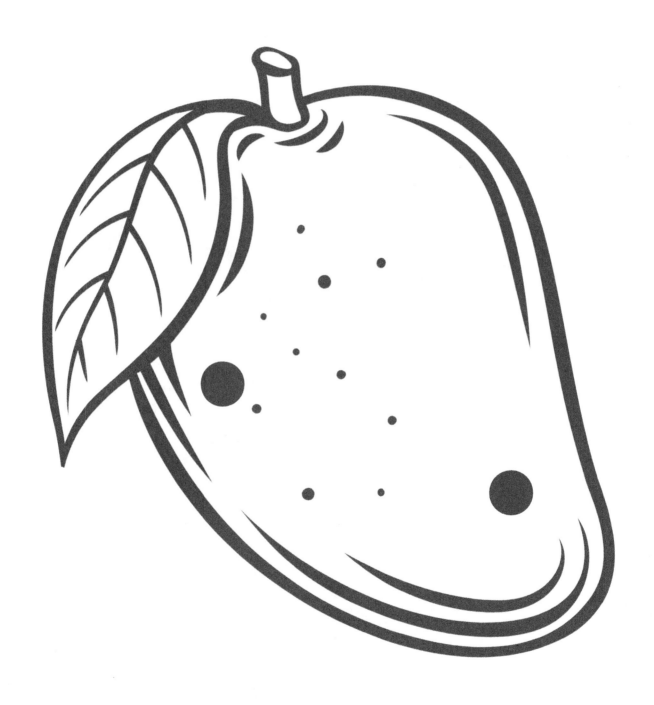

Mushroom

Avocado

Chili Pepper

Pomegranate

Beet

Apple

Artichoke

Pineapple

Cauliflower

Pear

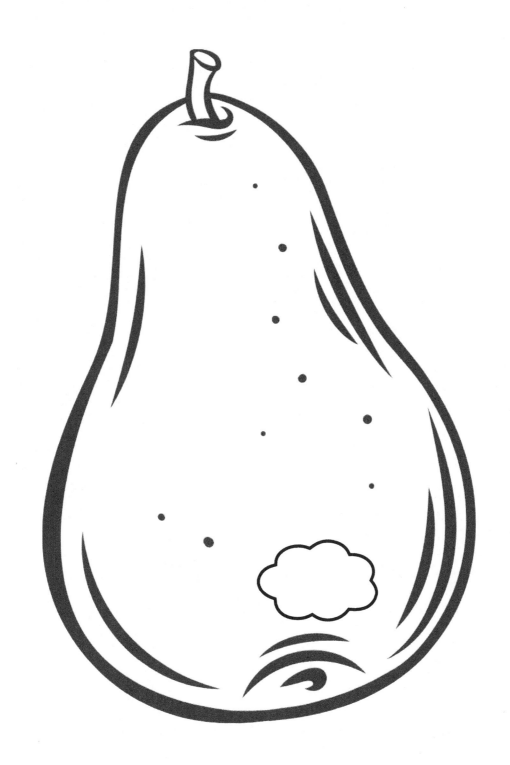

Cabbage

Mandarin

Eggplant

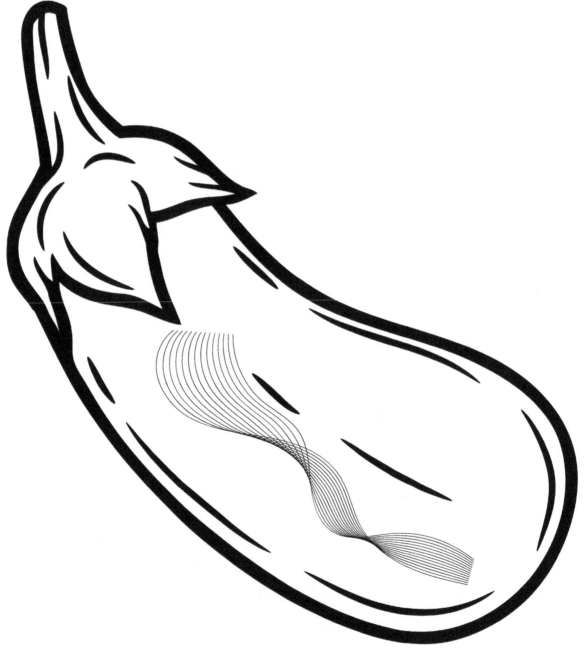

Raspberry

Pea

Lemon

Carrot

Dragon Fruit

Celery

Grapes

Ginger

Strawberry

Asparagus

Blueberry

Pumpkin

Peach

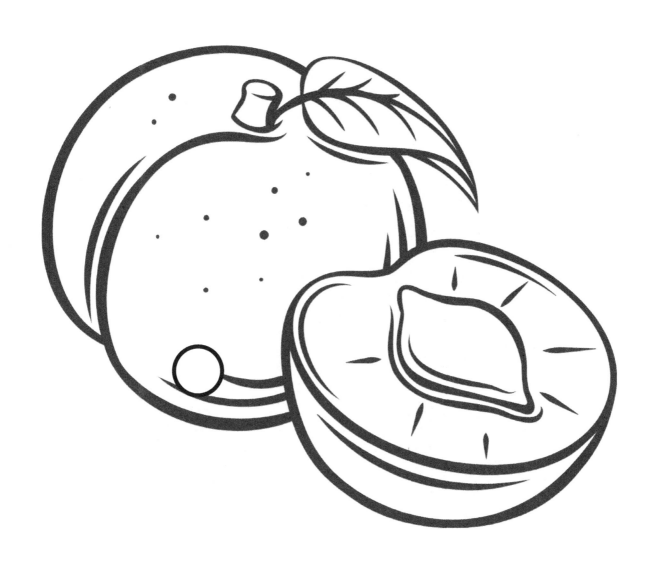

Corn

Cherry

Okra

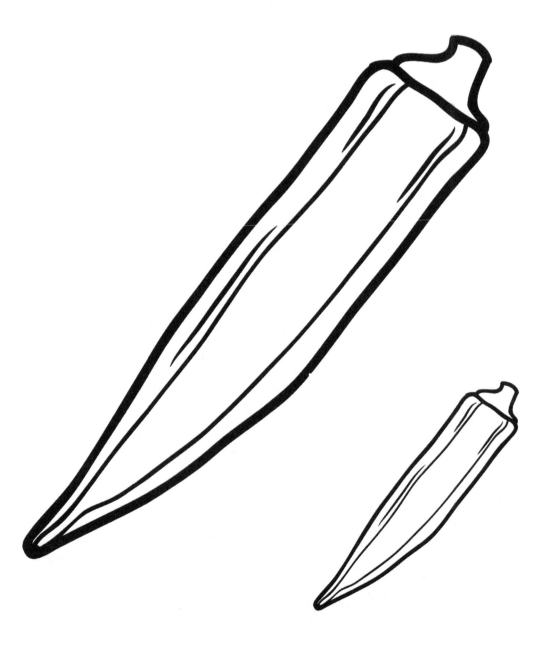

Watermelon

Garlic

Kiwi

Onion

Banana

Zucchini

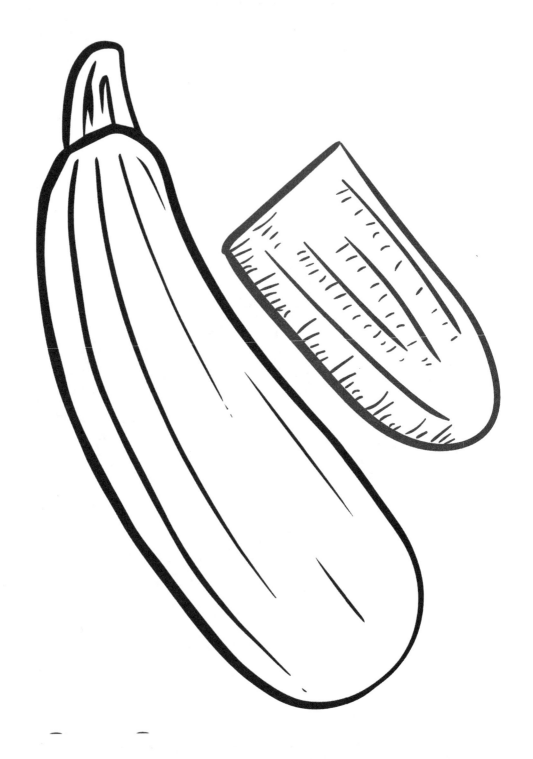

Pear

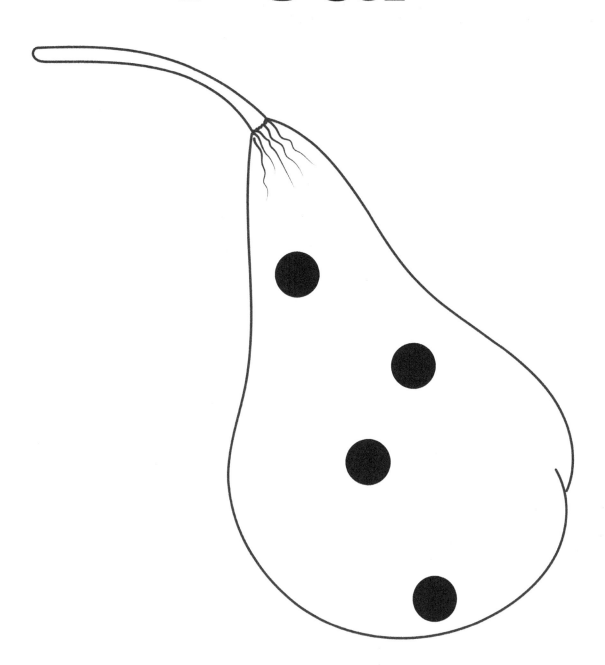

Coconut

Cucumber

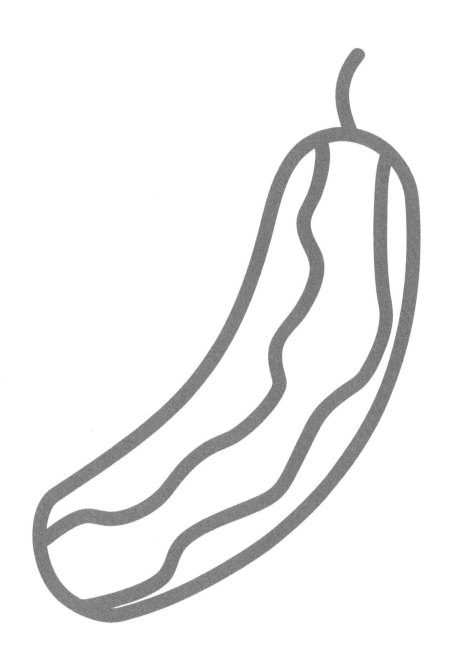

Orange

Bell Pepper

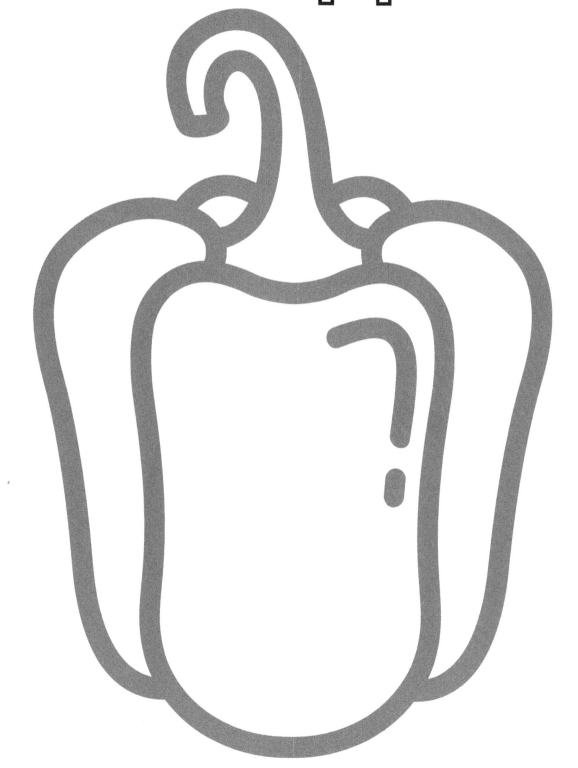

Dates

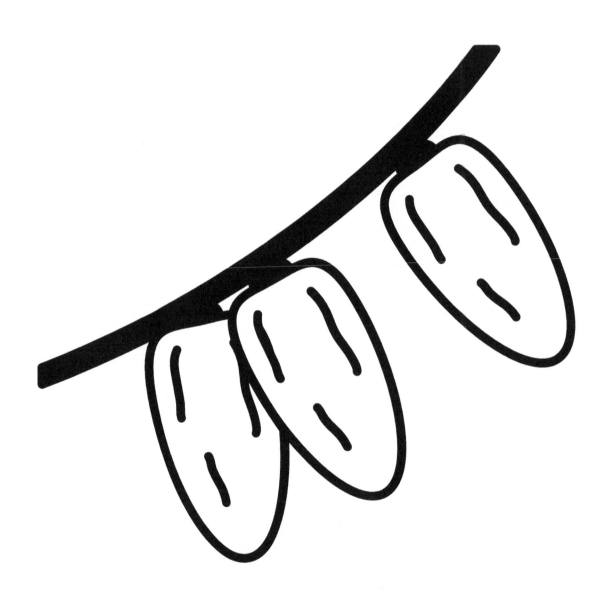

Spinach

Tamarind

Broccoli

Pear

Fig

Made in the USA
Middletown, DE
27 January 2023